1

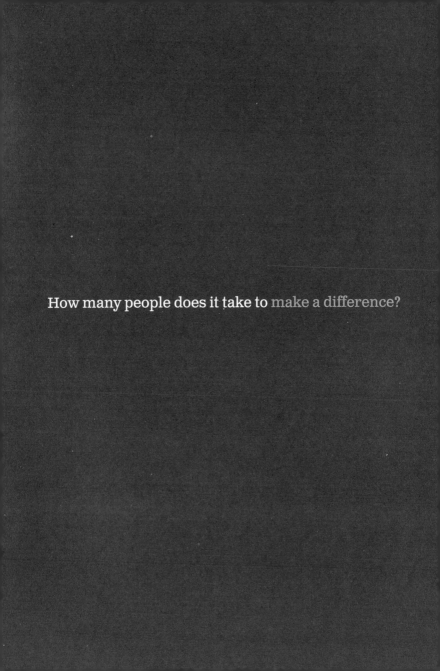

How many people does it take to make a difference?

The word "intention" comes from the Latin word *intendere*, which means "to stretch toward" something." Adopting a grand intention is what brings purpose, meaning, and significance to life.

The odds of your being born in this exact time and place are astronomical. People dream of winning the lottery, but you've already won the biggest lottery of all. It's called life. Savor it!

One
by
one,
we
can
be
the
better
world
we
wish
for.

_____

_____

_____

_____

_____

_____

_____

_____

_____

Your life can be a random string of incidents, accidents, or luck—or you can make it a thoughtfully

_____

_____

_____

_____

_____

_____

_____

_____

_____

_____

_____

charted course to touch the lives of others and make the difference only you can make in the world.

It's easy to become inspired. It's easy to find purpose and meaning. It's easy to bring more

_____

_____

_____

_____

_____

_____

_____

_____

_____

_____

oy and satisfaction into your life. All you have to do is focus on good ways to serve others.

_____

_____

_____

_____

_____

_____

_____

_____

_____

_____

_____

_____

_____

_____

_____

_____

_____

_____

_____

_____

_____

Everyone comes into the world with certain gifts designed to make the world a better place for

_____

_____

_____

_____

_____

_____

_____

_____

_____

_____

_____

themselves and others. An important question to ask: "What is my unique assignment on earth?"

HOW WILL YOU MAKE THE WORLD BETTER?

You are one of a kind. No one else in the world gets to be you, so you might as well make the most of it. Only you can become what you can become. Only you can touch the people you can touch.

_____

_____

_____

_____

_____

_____

_____

_____

There's a cause or an issue out there with your name on it. Something you care about.

_____

_____

_____

_____

_____

_____

_____

_____

_____

_____

_____

_____

omeplace where you can make a difference in a way that is unique to you. Find it. Follow it.

Families are homeless and hungry. Children are neglected and scared. Animals are abused an abandoned. Somebody should do something about it. Why not choose to be that somebody?

Listen closely

to your own

goodness

and act on it.

Visit the sick, dance with the elderly, take cancer patients to the store. Most problems seer ordinary" or "everyday," but that doesn't make solving them any less satisfying or significant.

Don't be afraid to give. Give joyfully. Give generously. Give because you can, because yo get to. Generosity—living big-heartedly—improves everyone's life, including your own.

Most of the good in the world isn't coming from a few, powerful people doing big things, but from illions of everyday people doing whatever they can, with whatever they have, wherever they are.

Whatever you do will matter. All you have to do is do it.

If you're a mechanic, fix a charity's truck. If you're a writer, write for a cause. If you're in sales, rais nds for something meaningful to you. If you can cook, make food for others. Give who you are.

Be a good-finder. Have high regards for all people. Seek out the best in every situation. Fir ways to put people up, not down. Look for the good in others and you will find it in yourself.

The word "vocation" comes from the Latin word *vocare*, which means "calling." How can ou find your calling? Look where your heart's desire intersects with what the world needs.

How do you want to be remembered?

There's so much suffering in the world, so much war, so many hungry children. How does one d the good? The answer is not to try to find it, but to create it. Create something good today.

It's often said that the three most pressing questions in life are, "Who am I, why am I here, an what do I want?" But a fourth question trumps the other three: "What can I do for others?"

1. Write down something you want to fix in the world. 2. Describe your vision of a successfu

utcome. 3. Break the vision into achievable goals. 4. Recruit kindred spirits. 5. Make it happen.

Do the right thing because it's right.

When you lend a hand, the world is more caring. When you stand up for what's right, the world i more just. When you inspire or encourage a child, the world is more hopeful. Everything counts.

"To whom much is given, much is expected." Every gift you've been given carries an equivale esponsibility. How can your gifts not only increase your own happiness, but that of the world?

Set aside a day each month to do something good, such as cleaning up a street. If you do ave time for a whole day, take half a day. If you don't have half a day, use your lunch hour.

Life is here and it is now.

Today
is the
day.

One of the greatest gifts we can give another person is our undivided attention... our genu

_____

_____

_____

_____

_____

_____

_____

_____

_____

terest. What would you hear if you focused on listening with intention for an entire day?

_____

_____

_____

_____

_____

_____

_____

_____

_____

_____

_____

_____

Research verifies that some of the happiest people are those who belong to large, positive social networks—great extended families, cohesive neighborhoods, or caring communities.

Make someone's day. Instead of spending $100 plus a $20 tip at an upscale restaurant, buy a $1 ndwich at your local sub shop and leave the same $20 tip. Your server will never forget you.

MAKE
SOMEONE'S
DAY.

From the Humans of New York website: As her husband lay dying, a woman asked him, "How a going to get along without you?" He said, "Take the love you have for me and spread it around."

_____

_____

_____

_____

_____

_____

_____

_____

_____

Think of a person—perhaps a teacher, coach, co-worker, neighbor, or friend—who had a

_____

_____

_____

_____

_____

_____

_____

_____

_____

_____

_____

_____

positive influence on your life, but who probably didn't realize it. It's not too late to thank them.

It's said that we'll be asked just two questions when we die. The answers determine if w get into heaven: "Have you found joy in life?" And, "Has your life brought joy to others?"

Use this interactive journal on its own or with the companion book,
1: How many people does it take to make a difference?

Discover all of the Life by the Numbers books and journals!

5: Where will you be five years
from today?

2: How will you create something
beautiful together?

7: How many days of the week
can be extraordinary?

10: What's on your top 10 list?